SOUP

Blanca Valencia, Dee Laffan & Mei Chin

CONTENTS

Ajiaco

INTRODUCTION

WHY SOUP?

While recording an episode for season 2 of our Spice Bags podcast, produced by Headstuff Podcast Network, on the topic of soup, we realised that while the three of us are from completely different backgrounds, cultures and upbringings, soup is a common ground. But why soup?

The answer is that soup connects us all. Everyone is passionately opinionated about their soups; maybe it's because of the role they played in our childhoods. We can all remember being served soup when we were feeling ill or having our favourite soup cooked for us, the one we still try to recreate today – its aromas transport us on nostalgic journeys. Soup is the ultimate ice breaker, the perfect meal no matter the occasion or guest. Soup is an elixir for any situation that life can throw at us. Soups highlight our traditions and tell the story of our food history. Soups define the stock from which we come.

During our work researching this book, we have shared many moments: countless debates, shopping for ingredients, cooking soups together and enjoying numerous bowls. Soup has taken us on a journey around the globe from the comfort of the communities within Ireland. We have learned so much from our contributors and together we have created a stock of memories and friends along the way. The collection of soups we have collated reflects individual cultures, memories and tastes. It's a true reflection of Irish food today and the people behind it.

Our soup exploration has surprised, shocked and delighted us. We are still students navigating the world of soups. Ultimately, this is a human journey, packed with memories, humour and revelations.

WHAT IS SOUP?

On our quest to broaden our views on soup and the people who make it, we discovered that soup has many diverse meanings, not one universal definition. To begin with, soup has a muddled language. This became apparent when Blanca was searching for an Indian soup and her Kerala-born neighbour, Ramya, informed her that there were no soups as such in her region. But when

Blanca asked what dals are, Ramya replied, 'Just dals, not soups, but they are from North India.' In Spain, a blended soup is called crema or puré. This clear divide is absent in modern-day Ireland, where a blended soup does not have another moniker.

This texture barrier between blended and chunky soups is sometimes insurmountable. In Dalian, China, where Blanca lived for two years, a blended soup (especially if made with tubers) can be slightly repugnant, as she learned when her daughters' ayi (nanny) refused to feed them blended soups. Mei's Chinese-American family is also partial to unblended soups, like Jewish chicken matzo ball soup, which are similar to traditional Chinese ones. Blended soups are absent from the traditional Italian soup repertory, which is unsurprising – who in their right mind would willingly submit themselves to a life tethered to a mouli (purée mill)?

An additional pitfall is the stew versus soup dilemma. Ajiaco, a Colombian soup made with potatoes, chicken and maize (page 10), is a main course, yet it's referred to as sopa in some texts and stew in others. In Nigeria, soups are thick, sauce-like dishes, so we added additional liquid to the traditional efo riro recipe (page 24), inexorably changing its essence. Ditto for Korean soondoobu, a stew or hot pot (page 51). Soup purists, please accept our apologies.

When it comes to deciphering soups, not speaking a language might be restrictive because it is via words that we build our understanding of how other cultures view their world. Languages and their essential cultural legacy are sometimes overlooked in an increasingly English-dominated world. Case in point: the lexicon of seaweed, or feamainn, in the Irish language is breathtakingly extensive, illuminating its importance, while our French neighbours are so desperate to preserve their language that the Académie Française is banning English words outright these days.

So for clarity's sake, let us state upfront that all the soups in this book defy easy classifications. We selected our soups in the same way you would friends, lovers and acquaintances. Some we have known and adored our whole lives, like Colombian ajiaco or gazpacho; others we have only just met and fallen in love with, like Danish hyldebærsuppe (elderberry soup); while others we'd like to learn more about, like Nigerian efo riro. But more importantly, soups have the power to transform and transport us. Perhaps they can do the same for you.

IMMIGRANT SOUP

Homesickness can strike a wanderer when least expected, and when it does, many of us long to soothe it with a bowl of something hot. When Mei first moved to Ireland, she craved chicken noodle soup. It had been a staple of her existence, whether poured from a Campbell's can or steaming in broth from a whole bird from the Jewish deli next door. In this regard, New York is better equipped than many places in the world, for it proffers soups – not just chicken noodle – for the plethora of people who flock there, giving the illusion of a hearth for those who have none. In contrast, Ireland can be a soup wasteland to a newcomer, with nothing to ward off its chill.

In Ireland, immigration numbers are growing and times are changing, and with them, the culinary climate. Years ago, there were few or no chillies, pulses or coriander. Now there are shops selling molokhia leaves and Thai aubergines, their shelves laden with spices, so scratching the immigrant itch is pretty easy. Nevertheless, when the nostalgia for one's country hits, one's favourite soup is often still *not* a three-minute journey away. We most desire soup when we are lonely and ailing. For Mei in New York City, soup was readily available although it might have taken someone else considerable time to produce it. As newcomers to a foreign country, some of us may find we have taken soup for granted in our past.

Many immigrants to Ireland still don't get their most-yearned-for soups on tap, so if the stores of cans and packets from suitcases have been used up (yes, soup hoarding is real), they must be duplicated. It's often a laborious task, but when we make soup, a world blooms – of memories, fragrances and faces. If we make it for others, it is a ladle of our lives that we share. The first restaurants in France sold broths that they claimed were restorative. By making a favourite soup, perhaps an immigrant can revive a small part of themselves, maybe something they weren't even aware they had missed.

WHAT SOUP MEANS TO ME

DEE

Growing up in Tipperary, every Saturday meant soup for lunch. We had a corner press beside our cooker with a shelf that swivelled outwards holding a Tupperware box containing a range of Knorr packet soups, neatly aligned in a row. Our menu consisted of two types of flavours. First there were the 'pure' flavours, such as thick chicken, cream of chicken, cream of mushroom, farmhouse vegetable and oxtail, which each could be made and enjoyed solely as one soup. Or we had the 'blended' selection, which introduced varieties like potato and leek; mushroom, cauliflower and broccoli; chicken and vegetable; and thick country vegetable. My father mastered the art of making his own custom blends by mixing and matching the different packets – the special Laffan blends.

The only time we had any other forms of soup was for special occasions. For example, at Christmas, a can of Campbell's mushroom soup was used to marry leftover turkey and ham into a casserole on St Stephen's Day, a tradition my sisters carried on from my mother, who died when I was six years old, mirroring her habitual way of using Christmas dinner leftovers in a one-pot wonder.

I didn't start making soup at home regularly until I was a college student, when I also relied on my dad's blended packet soup method, perfect for a student budget. After all, I am my father's daughter. Now, making chicken soup from the carcass is a weekly ritual in my home and I've added other favourites too, inspired by my travels, discovery of ingredients and friends. Writing this book has given me so many insights into what soups are forming part of modern Irish cuisine and being served in Irish homes today.

BLANCA

My dad, a Castilian engineer, is not impressed by appearances. He has built engineering projects in the toughest times and places, from the middle of the civil war in El Salvador to the Bolivian Altiplano. My mother, on the other hand, was a great beauty who studied Romance languages and dazzled everyone she met. She adored appearances and decorated herself in colourful, memorable attire.

My father's Castilian garlic soup was the antithesis to my Andalusian mother's gazpacho. Much like their personalities, these two soups reflect the fierce regional differences that define Spain and, by extension, my upbringing.

Castilian garlic soup is austere: water, bread, garlic and pimenton or paprika. It's a mainstay of the meseta norte, the northern plateau of Spain, where small-town winters can be shockingly cold and boring. Unknown outside of Spain, it is the quintessential soup of cold castles and historic military orders.

Gazpacho is cosmopolitan, featured in movies and TV and reinvented by chefs and food writers year after year. In one bowl or glass, you have the history of southern Spain from Rome to Al-Andalus (what the Arabs called Andalucía). The ingredients of fruity olive oil, tangy sherry vinegar, pungent garlic, sweet tomatoes and peppers from the 'New World' mix to create an original beauty.

I now realise that I am more garlic soup than gazpacho: serious, a bookworm, a lover of sobremesa (after-dinner talk). This is not to say that the little girl in me did not want at times to be the vibrant, red, cooling gazpacho that was my mother. In the confusion that is adulthood, I might sometimes be cold Castilian garlic soup and other times hot gazpacho, but every bit my parents' daughter.

MEI

As an ungainly Chinese latchkey child in Connecticut, Campbell's soup was elixir. With a few twists of a can opener in an empty house after school, I could, with Campbell's plethora of flavours – minestrone, tomato, chicken noodle – become a different girl. One summer, I ordered soupe à l'oignon in a Quebec restaurant. Spitting-hot cheese, seawater salty, it was, like a first sip of alcohol or initial cigarette, intoxicatingly adult. In the months that followed, I replicated it with Campbell's French onion, torn dinner rolls and supermarket Swiss cheese. When I ate it, I pictured myself beautiful and wearing pearls.

Soup is a coming of age, a metaphor and oft-sentimental calibration of self. Adultery soup: the minestrone at a pizza place called Naples where I went as a teenager with my stepfather-to-be and my still-married mother. Swimming with frozen vegetables, it registered as romantic and reckless. Zhou: after my birth father perished in a motorcycle accident, this Cantonese rice porridge, gamey with turkey and dried seafood, helped me come to terms with him, my Guangxi roots and the aspects of his character he had bequeathed to me.

In later life, much of my pleasure belongs to the soups of other people. Soup isn't fast; if someone makes it for you, you are together for hours and there is considerable conversation. As they put a pot on to boil and open their cabinets, they also offer up a sliver of their lives. When I drink another's soup, I can't help but feel an echo of the Campbell's girl I once was, sipping at existences not my own. It is also humbling, for I am reminded of how very little I know of life and the world.

WHEN IS THE RIGHT TIME TO HAVE SOUP?

If the exact definition of soup is elusive, we've noticed that soup serving times vary greatly among cultures too.

Don't we serve soup at the start of a meal? No. Soups are offered alongside a meal in many Asian cultures, while at weddings in Spain you can be served consommé in the middle of the night to keep the party going (as Blanca did to her Irish husband's friends and family, with mixed results).

Soups are just for lunch and dinner, right? This, too, proves to be problematic. Zhou, or congee (page 30), can be eaten for breakfast, while sinigang, a Filipino staple soup (page 48), can be had at any time of the day. This is also true of miso soups, which are a revered part of the Japanese morning table while we munch on Weetabix.

Is soup something that you can serve on its own at lunchtime? In Spain, where Blanca is from, you would not serve a simple soup for lunch (lunch is the main meal of the day), but in Ireland, where Dee hails from, it's perfectly normal. Hence, Blanca's first visits to her in-laws in Ireland left her perplexed and, needless to say, hungry.

GARNISHES

Let's face it – soup is a homely dish. If we eat with our eyes first, then soup needs some tarting up. However, sometimes garnishes are simply prettifying and possibly pretentious (flowers and popcorn, anyone?). Then there are soups like the sopa de tortilla on page 52 that is essentially a big bowl full of garnishes – herbs, limes, avocado and fried tortilla strips – held together by a broth. Below are some garnishes to consider.

CRACKERS This may be an American fetish, but we love saltines and oyster crackers – no other cracker will do. In Ireland, we make do with the water biscuit. Never, ever corrupt your bowl with a fancy cheese crisp or a Ritz.

CREAM Sometimes we're annoyed by that swirl of cream in a soup. Does it declare that the soup is creamy? However, in ajiaco (page 10), which is puritanical with its potatoes, corn and broth, the cream and caper garnishes are fundamental to turning this plain bowl into a swan.

CROUTONS They can be small, square and shop-bought or they can be thinly sliced and freshly toasted croûtes (our preference). While we agree, intellectually, that the square ones best belong in a salad, it's difficult not to slurp them. Croûtes, meanwhile, are a foundation for French onion soup (page 55) and play an integral role in the French fish soup, soupe de poisson.

EXTRA VIRGIN OLIVE OIL Across the Mediterranean Basin, people drizzle their soups with extra virgin olive oil. The oils' aromas and flavours range from pepper to grass and fruit. For us, our best oils are like wines; we care about the producer and its region. We are partial to early harvest estate-bottled varietals.

HERBS Parsley, mint, sorrel, tarragon and coriander are some of the fresh greens that bring a bit of garden to the bowl. The flowers of some herbs can also be used to embellish a soup and bring more flavour than a pansy or nasturtium.

SWEET BITS The crumble in the elderberry soup on page 33 changed us. We didn't think a sweet garnish was possible and it has shifted our perspective – for example, what about peanut brittle in a pumpkin soup?

8

STARCHY SIDES

Depending on where you're from in the world, soup can mean something completely different to you than it does to us. This also extends to how you serve soup, how you eat or drink it, when you choose to enjoy it or what you serve on the side. In recipes where a soup is more like a sauce or a stew, you'll often find a starchy side served to soak up the liquid and to balance intense flavours.

BREAD Bread is probably the most common starchy side served with soup in our part of the world, but the type of bread can be different. Sliced pan is popular in Ireland, but for specific soups, especially stew and chowder, brown soda bread is always served – with butter, it goes without saying. Sourdough is commonly served with soup in Poland and other Eastern European countries, while others have entrusted their soups to a crusty baguette, naan or roti.

PLANTAIN In Africa and the Caribbean, plantain is commonly served with soup. Plantains are members of the banana family but they are very starchy and must be cooked, so you certainly wouldn't want to eat one raw in the same way you would a banana! For savoury dishes like soup, plantains are cooked when they're green and either boiled or fried.

POLENTA Polenta isn't a common side dish with soup in most parts of the world, but it is sometimes used to thicken and add texture to a soup. However, some recipes call for serving diced fried polenta as a garnish, like croutons, or in larger pieces as a side. Georgian chakapuli (page 19) is served with ghomi, a traditional polenta dish consisting of coarse and fine cornmeal combined with water, with pieces of cheese placed in it to melt before being served.

RICE Soups from all corners of the globe are served with rice. In this book, you'll see it suggested for recipes from Brazil, Colombia, Korea, India, Nigeria and the Philippines. Rice is the perfect side to hold a soup or to add to it as you eat, soaking up the liquid and flavour combined. It makes for a heartier meal. In some countries, like Korea, the rice bowl is traditionally always served on the left.

AJIACO
COLOMBIAN CHICKEN, POTATO
& CORN SOUP

HE Mrs Patricia Cortés Ortiz, Colombian Ambassador to Ireland

SERVES 4–6

Colombia is blessed with ajiaco, a distinctive dish made with three different types of local potatoes, corn, chicken and a local herb called guascas (in Ireland, this is a weed called gallant soldier). One type of potato, Papa Criolla, is crumbly, buttery and imparts a yellow colour; while the other two – Pastusa, a floury one, and Sabanero, a waxy one – add different textures and flavours. We've called for three different types of potatoes that you can easily find in Ireland, but feel free to use only one or two types. The soup is garnished with cream, avocado and capers. Some ingredients, like the potatoes, corn, avocado and guascas, are native to Colombia, while others, like the capers, cream and chicken, were brought by the Spaniards. The result is a soup that reflects the mix of cultures that is Latin America. The Colombian ambassador to Ireland, HE Mrs Patricia Cortés Ortiz, not only shared this recipe but taught me how to cook it. Her freezer is always stocked with frozen Criolla potatoes imported via Spain, a staple she cannot live without. She serves it in the unique blue floral pattern ceramics of the town El Carmen de Viboral. Many thanks to my friend Miriam Abuin for arranging this. – BV

2 litres water

500g chicken or hen, on the bone

3 spring onions, left whole

4 garlic cloves, crushed

1 sprig of fresh thyme

4–6 sprigs of fresh coriander

4 medium waxy, red-skinned potatoes, peeled and thinly sliced

4 medium floury, yellow-skinned potatoes, peeled and thinly sliced

500g new potatoes, peeled and thinly sliced

4 chicken fillets

2 corn on the cob, cut in 3 pieces each

fine sea salt and freshly ground black pepper

Put the water in a stockpot with the chicken on the bone, spring onions, garlic, thyme and half of the coriander. Bring to the boil, then reduce the heat and simmer for 20 minutes.

Add the potatoes in batches, starting with the red-skinned waxy ones. Cook for 5 minutes, then add the yellow-skinned floury ones and cook for 5 minutes more. Add the new potatoes and cook for another 20 minutes, until the potatoes start to fall apart. (You could also put everything in a pressure cooker and cook it on high pressure for 15 minutes – see page 26).

Remove the spring onions from the pot. Pick the leaves from the rest of the coriander and add them to the pot along with the chicken fillets and corn. Simmer for 10–15 minutes, until the chicken fillets are cooked through.

TO SERVE:

150ml double cream or nata (see the glossary)

100g capers

2 avocados, skin on and cut into quarters

steamed or boiled white rice

Take the pot off the heat and remove the chicken on the bone and the fillets. Let them cool slightly, then shred with your hands or a fork and knife.

Check the consistency of the soup – the floury potato slices need to be broken up, not left whole. If needed, use a potato masher to break them down a little, but not too much. Check the seasoning and adjust the salt if necessary, remembering that the soup will be garnished with salty capers.

Stir the soup before serving, then ladle it into bowls, making sure every bowl has corn. Add the shredded chicken, a couple tablespoons of double cream or nata and some capers to the middle of each bowl. Serve with the avocado quarters and more capers and cream on the side. This soup is traditionally served with steamed or boiled white rice on the side.

LATIN AMERICAN POTATOES

For a close to authentic flavour in Ireland, use heirloom potatoes like Mayan Gold or Mayan Pink from Ballymakenny Farm in County Louth, potato farmers to the stars of the culinary world.

GUASCAS

Part of the distinctive taste of ajiaco comes from guascas (or gallant soldier, as it's called in Ireland). It imparts a faint bitter taste of herbs and artichoke that makes the soup unique. Gallant soldier grows wild in Ireland and the UK. It was introduced from Peru to Kew Gardens, where it seemingly escaped into the wild. We have substituted a little fresh coriander and thyme for the guascas here.

BEER & CHEESE SOUP WITH BACON & BROCCOLI

Imen McDonnell, United States

SERVES 4–6

Photographer, author, stylist and farmer Imen McDonnell (*The Farmette Cookbook*, Lens and Larder) hails from Wisconsin in the American Midwest. After years in New York, Minneapolis and Los Angeles, she landed in rural Limerick, embracing her inner pioneer with panache. Says Imen about this classic American heartland soup, 'It combines beer and dairy – a fitting blend, as the region is home to America's Dairyland and many breweries. I've added broccoli for a bit of a greening and bacon for a spot of smoke.' Imen's ideal beer for this soup is Wisconsin's Pabst Blue Ribbon, but it's not easily available here in Ireland. We suggest substituting it with a lager or pilsner. The best way to showcase this American beauty? In a bread bowl, of course. – MC

180g smoked bacon lardons

1 small onion, finely chopped

1 celery stick, finely chopped

1 medium leek, thinly sliced

2 large garlic cloves, finely chopped

1½ tsp dried rosemary

350ml American-style lager or German pilsner

600ml chicken stock

60g unsalted butter

40g plain flour

230g mature Cheddar cheese, grated

100g smoked Cheddar cheese, grated

250ml double cream

1 tbsp mustard powder

300g broccoli florets, steamed and coarsely chopped

1½ tsp chilli flakes

fine sea salt and freshly ground black pepper

Cook the bacon lardons in a large saucepan over a medium heat until crisp, then transfer to a plate using a slotted spoon.

Add the onion, celery, leek, garlic and rosemary to the fat that rendered out of the bacon in the saucepan and cook for 7–8 minutes, stirring, until softened. Add half of the beer and simmer for about 5 minutes, until reduced by half. Pour in the chicken stock and bring to a simmer.

Melt the butter in a separate small saucepan over a medium heat. Add the flour and cook, stirring, until lightly browned. Whisk this roux into the soup, stirring until incorporated, and bring back to a simmer. Cook for about 8 minutes, until thickened.

Add the cheeses, cream, mustard powder and the remaining beer and cook for about 5 minutes, stirring occasionally, until thick and creamy. Stir in the bacon lardons (save a few crispy bits for garnish), steamed broccoli and chilli flakes, then season to taste with salt and pepper.

If you're serving the soup in a bread bowl, slice the top off the boule. Hollow out the inside of the loaf, leaving

TO SERVE:

1 medium-sized boule loaf
or 4 small boule loaves
(optional)

chopped fresh chives

the crust intact (reserve the insides for stuffing or bread pudding), then ladle the soup inside. One medium bread bowl should hold enough soup for four people; otherwise, you can do this with four small individual loaves.

Garnish with chopped chives and crisp bacon lardons and serve hot.

ALCOHOL IN SOUP

Wine, spirits and, in this case, beer give an extra dimension to soup, as they do to so many other dishes. In this recipe you want to cook off the alcohol, however, so that you have all the flavour and none of the dissipation. But there are certain soups where you add the alcohol at the end, like a dash of sherry in the Spanish consomé al Jerez. As Julia Child said, 'I enjoy cooking with wine. Sometimes I even put it in the food.'

BORSCH
UKRAINIAN BEETROOT SOUP

Alexandra (Sasha) Shyskina, Ukraine and the US

SERVES 4–6

Sasha is a Ukrainian-American food photographer based in Dublin. As newcomers to Dublin, Sasha and I met in the Triggerfish cookshop in Blackrock, where she photographed and filmed some of the cooking classes and cookware. Sasha has great talent and determination and faced the prospect of starting from scratch in a new city with optimism and a smile.

Sasha has shared her mother's recipe for borsch ('No T, please!' Sasha says), a treasured heirloom that can make us reflect on the culinary heritage of Ukraine, where this soup hails from. Borsch, a light beetroot and meat soup, is well-known but it has its little tricks and tips. For instance, I had never heard of zazharka, the Ukrainian sofrito that you can add to borsch, but my Ukrainian neighbour, Serhiy, prefers to omit it because of the oil. He also despairs at how often a floury potato can ruin borsch. In addition, some cooks, such as Sasha's mother, blanch their beetroot because they prefer a less pink soup (something I personally adore). – BV

FOR THE STOCK:

500g beef oxtail or short ribs

1 onion, cut in half

1 carrot, roughly chopped

1 tbsp fine sea salt or to taste

2 litres water

FOR THE ZAZHARKA:

2 tbsp vegetable or sunflower oil

1 onion, finely diced

1 medium carrot, grated

2 tbsp tomato purée

200ml water

To make the stock, put the meat, onion, carrot and salt in a pot and cover with the water. Bring to the boil, removing the fat and impurities that rise to the top. Reduce the heat and simmer until the meat is tender – this could be anywhere between 1 and 2 hours depending on the cut and type of meat. (You can reduce the cooking time by using a pressure cooker and cooking the stock for 30–40 minutes at high pressure; see page 26). Remove the onion and carrot, then set the stock aside.

While the stock is cooking, make the zazharka, which is essentially a Ukrainian sofrito. Heat the oil in a sauté pan over a medium heat. Add the onion and carrot and sauté for about 5 minutes, until soft. Whisk the tomato purée with the water in a separate small bowl, then add this to the zazharka. Simmer for about 15 minutes, until thickened.

To finish the soup, add the beetroot and onion to the pot with the stock and cook for 15 minutes, then add the potatoes and cook for another 10 minutes, until softened.

TIP

You can replace the homemade stock with shop-bought beef stock, but keep in mind that the stock used in borsch is a light meat one, so dilute it accordingly.

FOR THE SOUP:

1 large beetroot, peeled and cut into matchsticks

1 large onion, diced

4 medium waxy potatoes, peeled and cubed

¼ cabbage, shredded

1 red pepper, sliced

2 garlic cloves, crushed

4 bacon rashers, chopped and fried

fine sea salt and freshly ground black pepper

TO SERVE:

100g sour cream

1 bunch of fresh dill, chopped

soft white rolls or rye bread

garlic butter

Add the zazharka, cabbage and red pepper and bring to the boil. Simmer for 5 minutes, until the cabbage and pepper are cooked. Add the crushed garlic, fried bacon and salt and pepper to taste and simmer for a few minutes more.

Serve each bowl with a generous dollop of sour cream and plenty of chopped fresh dill, with soft bread rolls or rye bread spread with garlic butter on the side.

BOTWINKA
POLISH BEETROOT SOUP WITH LEAVES

Kamila Bystrzonowska, Poland

SERVES 4

The Polish word *botwinka* literally means 'a soup made of beets with leaves' and that is precisely what this recipe is. However, this version was given to us by Kamila, co-owner of the award-winning Momo restaurant in Waterford City, and it is very much made to her tastes. Kamila is passionate about vegetables and foraging, which is apparent on her restaurant menu and on the plate. 'There are a few versions of beetroot soup and every cook has their own take. This soup is everything I like about beetroot soups. It's the combination of my favourite flavours – I love the umami flavour and wild mushrooms in this and beetroot kvass adds a sour flavour. This soup represents summer for me. Baby beetroot and greens, dill – this is what I wait for all winter.'

This soup is a paradox, at once fresh and hearty. The keys to its tastiness are the wild mushrooms in the stock and the dill garnish. As Kamila says, 'There is no such thing as too much dill!' – DL

FOR THE STOCK:

2 carrots, chopped

1 parsnip, chopped

½ celeriac, peeled and diced

½ leek, chopped

2 garlic cloves, chopped

3–4 whole allspice

2 bay leaves

2 litres water

To make the stock, put all the ingredients in a large saucepan over a high heat and bring to the boil. Turn the heat down and simmer for 1–2 hours, until the vegetables are completely cooked and the water has reduced – you need 1 litre of stock for this recipe. Sieve the stock through a colander. Alternatively, you can use 1 litre of shop-bought vegetable stock.

Meanwhile, wash the dried wild mushrooms and soak them in a bowl of cold water for 30 minutes, then strain through a fine mesh sieve (they can have a lot of sand). Set aside.

Wash and peel the beetroot, carrots, potatoes and parsnip. Remember to put gloves on when you're preparing beetroot! Chop all the vegetables into small cubes, around 1cm or smaller. Chop the beetroot leaves, including the stems, into 5mm pieces.

Heat the butter or oil in a large saucepan. Add the beetroot (not the leaves or stems at this point), carrots, potatoes, parsnip and vegetable stock and bring to the boil. Reduce the heat to medium and cook for around

FOR THE SOUP:

20g dried wild mushrooms

2 medium-sized beetroot
(with the beetroot leaves, if
possible)

2 carrots

2–3 waxy potatoes

1 parsnip

1 tbsp butter or vegetable
oil

fine sea salt and freshly
ground black pepper

225g broccoli florets
(optional)

115g fresh or frozen garden
peas

3 garlic cloves, chopped

300ml beetroot kvass or
concentrated beetroot juice
(see the glossary)

a handful of fresh dill,
chopped

TO SERVE:

4 hard-boiled eggs

sourdough bread and butter

30 minutes, until the beetroot and carrots are soft but still with a little bite. Taste and add salt and pepper if needed.

Add the broccoli (if using), peas, garlic and beetroot leaves and stems and continue cooking for 5–7 minutes, until just cooked through.

Turn off the heat and stir in the beetroot kvass or concentrated beetroot juice. If you're using kvass don't bring it back to the boiling point, as the soup would lose its beautiful deep colour and the nutritive value of the fermented juice. Bring it to the boil only if using concentrated beetroot juice. Taste again and add salt and pepper if needed. Add lots of chopped dill at this point.

Serve with a hard-boiled egg and a nice thick slice of sourdough bread with butter.

A BORSCHT BY ANY OTHER NAME

Borscht (also spelled barszcz in Poland or borsch, borsht or bortsch) is a vibrant, often sour beetroot soup originating in Ukraine. We've included a recipe for Ukrainian borsch (page 14), where it's pronounced borshtch with no audible *t* at the end. This recipe for botwinka (which is a summer borscht) is Kamila's own version, with flavours of Christmas barszcz in it, like her grandmother used to make.

'I remember Christmas barszcz so well,' Kamila says. 'This soup is filling, fresh and full of flavour and herbs. It gives you a lovely comforting and feel-good feeling – you know that you are eating something healthy and nutritious, and delicious too. My grandmother used to make a very similar soup, but I never got the recipe so I created my own version. It is a meal in a bowl – an egg adds protein, potatoes fill your belly and vegetables just make you feel good. This soup tastes like Poland for me.'

CHAKAPULI
GEORGIAN LAMB STEW WITH HERBS

Nino Maschkhashvii, Georgia

SERVES 4–6

When Nino Maschkhashvii's daughters wanted to go to university in Georgia she could not afford it, so she left her job as a schoolteacher in Rustavi and came to Dublin to work as a childminder and cleaner. Nino, who is passionate about folktales, history and ballad songs, also loves to cook, so those who know her may be surprised by a container of her homemade lobo bean stew or a batch of her mchadi, a fried, puffed cornbread. Nino's chakapuli lamb stew swims with tarragon and coriander, is flavoured with wild green plums and spiced with tkemali, a condiment of more green plums and coriander that could be considered the nation's ketchup.

This soup is typical of the sophisticated, poetic, bewitching Georgian cuisine, whose fruits, spices and flowers (like the white jonjoli blossom, which is salted and served in salad) reflect the country's long-standing place on the Spice Route. Georgia, which shares borders with Turkey, Russia, Azerbaijan and Armenia, is the home of Jason's Golden Fleece, the creator of polyphonic/harmonic music (there would be no Mozart operas or Beach Boys without it) and, many claim, the birthplace of wine, where it was produced as far back as 6000 BC.

Chakapuli is famously a spring dish, for that is when the wild green plums can be harvested and there is baby lamb. Should you be lucky enough to have baby lamb, your cooking time will be shorter. Put the wild plums in whole – part of the joy in eating them is spitting out their pits. Traditionally this is served with ghomi, a Georgian polenta. – MC

1kg lamb stewing meat or lamb neck

100g fresh tarragon, roughly chopped

100g fresh coriander, roughly chopped

100g spring onions, roughly chopped

20g wild green plums (optional; see the glossary)

400ml white wine

fine sea salt and freshly ground black pepper

3 tbsp tkemali or to taste (see the glossary)

Put a heavy-based pot with a lid over a medium-high heat. Put in the lamb and all the other ingredients except the tkemali. Season with salt and pepper, cover with the lid and bring to the boil. Reduce the heat to medium-low, then add the tkemali. Season with salt and pepper, cover and simmer for 2 hours, until the lamb is completely tender.

Taste the soup – if you want more tart fruit flavour, you can add one or two more spoonfuls of tkemali, especially if you haven't used any wild green plums. Adjust the seasoning with a little more salt and pepper if needed and serve.

CHERRY GAZPACHO

Blanca Valencia, Spain

SERVES 6–8

During my childhood summer vacations in Andalusia, gazpacho was only a boring tomato drink. It wasn't until I watched Pedro Almodóvar's movie *Women on the Verge of a Nervous Breakdown*, where the protagonist artfully drinks bright-red gazpacho (laced with Valium!) out of a glass, wears a red jacket and talks on a red phone, that its glamorous possibilities unfolded. However, it was Spanish chef Dani Garcia's fruit gazpachos that cemented this dish in my culinary repertoire. Let me warn you, though, that nothing kills a gazpacho buzz more than lousy olive oil and subpar vinegar. I will not let anything but early harvest extra virgin olive oil (preferably the Picual varietal) come near my gazpacho, and neither should you. Also, no black pepper, please! It detracts from its delicacy. – BV

1kg ripe tomatoes, coarsely chopped (or if out of season, use cherry tomatoes)

400g pitted cherries, coarsely chopped, plus extra or chopped strawberries to garnish

100g day-old crusty bread, sliced and soaked in water for 1 hour

½ small onion, chopped

⅛ green pepper, sliced

1 small garlic clove, sliced

100ml early harvest extra virgin olive oil (see the intro)

4 tsp sherry vinegar

fine sea salt

Blend all the ingredients except the olive oil, vinegar and salt until smooth. You might need to do this in batches. Sieve through a medium-mesh strainer and discard the solids. Season with the olive oil, vinegar and salt, mixing it well. Chill overnight to allow the flavours to develop.

Serve chilled in a bowl or glass garnished with a sliced strawberry or chopped cherries. Gazpacho freezes very well and can last for a couple of months in the freezer.

SOUP VESSELS

Soups come in many vessels, from ceramics to lacquerware, which adds an additional layer of meaning to an already symbolic dish. The vessel can be a family heirloom, an acquired pricey soup tureen, a bowl made of bread or coconut or a humble slow cooker. Here are some of our favourites.

LA CHAMBA CLAY POTS (COLOMBIA)

In Colombia, many cooks like to serve ajiaco in the iconic black clay bowls of La Chamba. These handmade pots with a natural shine can be found in posh ceramics stores in Madrid, Paris and London. They connect the soup to ancestral traditions of the pre-Columbian inhabitants.

LACQUERWARE (JAPAN)

Japanese lacquerware is used to serve miso soup. This technique dates back thousands of years and uses wood and sap to create naturally insulating bowls. The delicacy of the bowl matches the soup's elegance. Miso and other dainty clear soups are served with a lid on.

FAJALAUZA CERAMICS (SPAIN)

In Granada, where Blanca's mother's family is from, you can buy gazpacho sets made in traditional blue and white ceramic. They often feature a pomegranate, the emblem of the city. In the past, this was something grandmothers had hidden in their kitchen cupboards. The newfound appreciation for artisan work in Spain means that these humble bowls are now made in a myriad of colours and command steeper prices.

WHITE PORCELAIN SOUP TUREENS

Nothing dresses up a soirée more than a soup tureen and a white tablecloth. Soup tureens were fabulously commissioned in all types of materials to impress the guests of the very rich and aristocratic families across Europe. In the 1970s they were still quite popular, but now are sadly in disuse. Look for them in second-hand stores and parish fêtes – you might find a nice French lion head one for just a few euro.

CULLEN SKINK
SCOTTISH SMOKED HADDOCK &
POTATO SOUP

Sally Barnes, Scotland

SERVES 4

Sally Barnes, owner of West Cork's Woodcock Smokery, smoked her first fish in a tea chest when she was a dewy fisherman's bride. Her ruby-complected salmon is internationally coveted, as are her haddock and mackerel. Sally loves wild fish for the gorgeous flavour of its flesh. Furthermore, she maintains this principle in her work because it respects both the sea and the people who catch them. 'I have a reverence for all wild things,' Sally says, 'how they manage to live their lives, despite human interventions and problems.' Her cullen skink is a Scottish comfort soup of haddock and potatoes but, like Sally, it's also a wee bit wild. A lifelong forager, Sally says, 'I sometimes use three-cornered leeks in the skink because they're fresh and on my doorstep.' We love the sweet, slightly pungent whiff that they lend. If you can't find three-cornered leeks, use the more readily available garlic scapes, ramps or garlic chives, or you can leave them out entirely. – MC

250–300g undyed smoked haddock

25g butter or extra virgin olive oil

1 large onion, thinly sliced

2 floury potatoes, peeled and chopped into medium cubes

500ml milk

a handful of three-cornered leeks or garlic scapes, finely chopped (optional; see the intro)

fine sea salt and freshly ground black pepper

a handful of fresh parsley or dill, chopped

TO SERVE:

good crusty bread and butter

Skin the smoked haddock and remove any bones. Although most smoked haddock is filleted, you will still find a few bones. Cut the fish into 10cm chunks and set aside.

Melt the butter or oil in a saucepan over a medium heat. Add the onion and gently sauté until it's translucent. Add the chopped potatoes, then stir in the milk. Reduce the heat to medium-low and let the soup come up to a simmer. Be careful not to let the soup boil or the milk will curdle. Simmer for 15 minutes.

Stir in the haddock pieces and bring everything back to a simmer. Cook for 5 minutes more, until the potatoes are soft and falling apart. Add the three-cornered leeks or garlic scapes (if using) and cook for another minute. Taste the soup before you add any seasoning. The fish is salty so the skink may not need more, but add freshly ground black pepper to taste.

Garnish with chopped parsley or dill and serve with crusty bread and butter.

EFO RIRO
NIGERIAN SPINACH STEW
Edizemi Onilenla, Nigeria

SERVES 4

Edizemi – or Emi, as she likes to be called – is a food entrepreneur and the founder of Mansion Foods, which houses the brand Mama Shee, bringing the rich taste of Nigerian cuisine to Ireland. I first tasted Emi's food in Merrion Square in Dublin, where Mama Shee is a vendor at the market on Thursdays. I was a fan immediately. Spicy jerk chicken, the smoky flavours of jollof rice and the sweetness of fried plantain – her food is as vivacious and ebullient as she is.

Efo riro, or Nigerian spinach stew, is essentially a sauce that you can add any meat or fish to and it is often served with plantain or rice. This recipe is Emi's own that she kindly taught me. A beautiful tomato base packed with Nigerian flavours, it packs a punch in the best way. – DL

300g stewing lamb, diced

1 litre chicken stock

3 fresh red chillies, stems removed

1 Scotch bonnet chilli, stem removed

2 large sweet red peppers, stems removed

1 red pepper, stem removed

1 x 400g tin of chopped tomatoes

2 tbsp African pure palm oil (see the glossary)

2 onions, diced

250g fresh spinach, shredded

1 tbsp all-purpose vegetable seasoning (see the glossary)

1 tbsp crayfish powder (see Africa's Finest Dried Fish in the glossary)

200g fresh prawns

TO SERVE (OPTIONAL):

steamed or boiled white rice or plantain

Put the lamb and chicken stock in a pressure cooker and cook for 20 minutes, until the lamb is tender and almost falling apart. If you don't have a pressure cooker, you can simmer the lamb in a saucepan on a low heat for 45 minutes. Drain off the stock and set the lamb aside.

Meanwhile, put all the chillies and peppers (including the seeds) and the tin of tomatoes in a blender and blitz until you have a sauce consistency.

Put the palm oil in a deep pan over a very high heat. Add the onions and cook for 2 minutes, then pour in the chilli and pepper sauce. Turn down the heat slightly and simmer for 5 minutes.

Rinse the spinach in a colander under the hot water tap so that it wilts slightly. Squeeze out the excess water.

Stir the vegetable seasoning and crayfish powder into the sauce, then add the prawns along with the cooked lamb and the wilted spinach. Cook for about 5 minutes, until the prawns are done.

Serve the soup immediately, either on its own or with rice or plantain.

NIGERIAN INGREDIENTS

In learning to make this recipe and spending time in the kitchen with Emi, we also learned a lot about Nigerian cuisine and commonly used ingredients. Here are three we want to highlight.

DRIED FISH

Before the introduction of stock cubes to West Africa, dried fish were commonly used to add flavour to food. These intensely flavoured fish not only add a blast of umami to dishes that is unique to this cuisine, but also texture. Emi's original recipe uses dried lizard fish, but we opted for fresh prawns instead. However, if you want to relish the full intensity of this Nigerian sauce's flavour, add a tablespoon of dried lizard fish to this recipe.

PEPPER SOUP MIX

Another very popular and distinctly flavoured Nigerian soup is pepper soup, which can be made using fish or any meat. When trying out recipes for this cookbook, we made a goat pepper soup with Emi that was super simple. The pepper soup mix is shop-bought and is a mix of ground white peppercorns, cloves, ginger and garlic (different brands' ingredients vary).

POWDERED STOCKS & SEASONINGS

It's common in Nigerian cuisine to use powdered stocks and seasonings as base flavours that add complexity to the dishes.

THE PRESSURE COOKER:
A SPEEDY AFFAIR

Electric and traditional pressure cookers are a godsend for anyone who is short on time or money or concerned about the impact our cooking has on the environment.

When you use a pressure cooker, the cooking time of most recipes is reduced by 70%. When it comes to meat stocks, what takes hours on the stovetop takes 20–30 minutes in a pressure cooker. This is especially important in the recipes for ajiaco (page 10), borsch (page 14), efo riro (page 24) and turkey zhou (page 30). Vegetable soups can also be made in a pressure cooker.

Pressure cookers also speed up legumes: you can cook legumes in a quarter of the time with a pressure cooker. If you've ever eaten beans from a tin or glass jar, you know how much waste they produce compared to dried legumes. One cup of dried beans equals approximately four cups of cooked beans, so this means you can spend more money on high-quality organic legumes rather than low-cost canned ones.

No matter how much people complain about soaking beans overnight, it's an easy step. In a pinch, you can even cook unsoaked beans in a pressure cooker – just cook them a little longer. A pressure cooker also allows you to buy cheaper cuts of meat that take hours to cook on the stovetop and which make delicious stews and soups.

The electric Instant Pot, our favourite pressure cooker, is convenient because it does not use gas and can be hooked up to solar panels or renewable electric sources. It's not pretty – it's tough-looking, like the small, ugly brother of R2D2.

Flans, cheesecakes, jams, whole grains, rice – all can be cooked in a pressure cooker. Check out food writer Catherine Phipps's informative and chic books on pressure cooking if you want to learn more.

EVEREST GARLIC SOUP

Dee Laffan, Ireland

SERVES 4

In 2017 I trekked to Everest Base Camp, which was an incredible, transformational experience. Food is a vital part of your journey – you burn about 5,000 calories a day trekking at high altitudes, so you need to replenish often. All meals started with soup, which we were served in the tea lodges along the route. Garlic soup is important because it helps you avoid altitude sickness. While I had never tried it before, it became a comfort food that I longed for. Often served with a thinner consistency, this creamy version was my favourite that soothes me to this day. – DL

100g unsalted butter

2 brown onions, chopped

5–6 garlic cloves, coarsely chopped

4 medium Orla potatoes (or any waxy yellow potato), peeled and chopped

fine sea salt and freshly ground black pepper

TO SERVE:

Nepalese roti, Indian chapati or flatbreads

Melt the butter in a saucepan over a medium heat. Add the onions, reduce the heat slightly and sweat for 8–10 minutes, until softened. Stir in half the garlic and all the potatoes and season with salt and pepper. Cook for 2 minutes, then cover with water and simmer until the potatoes are tender.

Meanwhile, sprinkle some sea salt on the remaining garlic on a chopping board. With the back of a sharp knife, push down and drag the garlic over and over, crushing it to a smooth paste.

Remove the soup from the heat and liquidise using a hand-held blender or food processor. If the soup is too thick, add more water – it should have a lighter, thin soup consistency. Stir the garlic paste into the soup, then taste and adjust the seasoning.

Serve with roti, chapati or flatbreads.

HARIRA
MOROCCAN SOUP WITH CHICKPEAS, LENTILS, VERMICELLI & LAMB

Aziz Krouch, Morocco

SERVES 4

Aziz is the head chef of Marrakech by Mindo on Dublin's Capel Street. He began as a chef at Marrakech's glamorous La Mamounia, then swanned through Paris and New York City before landing in Dublin, exhausted from that cosmopolitan life. Soft-spoken and erudite, Aziz is a marvellous raconteur, whether he's describing his grandmother making warqa (pastry) in the Atlas Mountains, the appropriate pairing of fruit and meat in a tagine or the role of tea and spice trading routes in history. Harira is a soup for all seasons, but it's a crucial element of Moroccan Ramadan, where people break their all-day fast at sundown. Succulent with lentils and lamb, harira lines the stomach at the beginning of the Ramadan meal and is served with something sweet, like dates and pastries. – MC

30g brown lentils

1 large bunch of fresh coriander, chopped

1 large bunch of fresh flat-leaf parsley, chopped

2 celery sticks, thinly sliced at an angle

2 ripe tomatoes, quartered

2 tbsp olive oil

450g lamb neck, bone in and cut into small pieces

1 onion, finely diced

1 tsp ground ginger

1 tsp ground coriander

1 tsp ground black pepper

1 vegetable stock pot

¼ tsp saffron (or ¼ tsp ground turmeric)

30g plain flour

50ml water

Soak the lentils in a small bowl of water for 1 hour, then drain and rinse.

Put the coriander, parsley, celery and tomatoes in a food processor and blitz until finely blended but not puréed – about the consistency of a pesto.

Heat the oil in a large heavy-based pot over a low heat. Add the lamb, raise the heat to medium-high and fry for 5–7 minutes, stirring from time to time, until the bones begin to brown. Add the onion, cover the pot and sweat for 5 minutes.

Add half of the herb mixture to the pot along with the spices (if you're using turmeric instead of saffron, add it now), soaked and drained lentils, vegetable stock pot and enough water to cover everything generously. Bring to the boil, then reduce the heat to medium, cover the pot and let the soup gently simmer for 15 minutes. If you're using saffron instead of turmeric, put the saffron in a small heatproof dish (or wrap it in tin foil) and sit it on top of the lid to warm. Check that the lentils are cooked – if not, cook for a couple minutes more, until they are done.

25g tomato purée

1 x 400g tin of chickpeas, drained and rinsed

25g fine vermicelli noodles, broken into 10cm lengths

fine sea salt and freshly ground black pepper

TO GARNISH (OPTIONAL):

hard-boiled eggs, halved

12 dates

lemon wedges

Meanwhile, in a separate small bowl, make a silky paste by whisking the flour and water together.

Stir the tomato purée into the pot, then reduce the heat to medium-low. Add the flour paste, chickpeas and the rest of the herb mixture. Cook for a couple of minutes, stirring. Add the vermicelli and the warmed saffron (if using) and cook for 2 more minutes. Make sure that you keep stirring once you've added the flour paste, as the soup will thicken. If needed, thin it with a little water. Taste for salt and adjust if necessary. This is a family-style recipe so there is no need to remove the lamb bones, but Aziz does remove them shortly before serving if he makes this for the restaurant.

Serve each bowl of harira with a halved hard-boiled egg, three dates and a lemon wedge.

DATES AND ODD NUMBERS

Both dates and odd numbers are important to the Islamic and the Moroccan traditions. Odd numbers, especially the prime numbers 3, 5 and 7, repeat themselves in the Quran; for instance, there is a five-time call to prayer each day and the prophet Mohamed began his non-holiday mornings by eating seven dates. Dates are a fundamental fruits in much of the Islamic world. Aziz pragmatically muses, 'In Morocco we have dates year round, as opposed to any other fruits, which are seasonal.'

At Ramadan, when the fast is broken at sundown, Aziz, and many others in Morocco, choose to begin their meal with three dates and a hard-boiled egg. The candy-sweet fruits are packed with fibre and line the stomach. Three dates is a good number, especially before a Ramadan feast, for they waken the palate without inviting gluttony.

HUO JI ZHOU
CHINESE TURKEY CONGEE
WITH DRIED SHRIMP

Mei Chin, United States

SERVES 4–6

As a child in Connecticut, I turned my nose up at my Cantonese father's day-after-Thanksgiving turkey zhou (stewed breakfast rice porridge). Only as an adult did I come to terms with my Chinese side, which includes having a cupboard that smells like dried fish, and embrace turkey zhou. It follows a day of gluttony, is soothing and savoury, but it also has the mild funk of a bird the day after. Moreover, this zhou is part of my heritage. I am an American-born Chinese, and this is Thanksgiving turkey steeped with rice.

Turkey zhou should be ivory (not white) and spiked with brine from dried seafood, salted egg, pickles and pork floss. Traditionally, zhou is served with youtiao (think salty churros). If these aren't available, shop-bought Yorkshire puddings are a wonderful accompaniment. – MC

20g raw peanuts (optional)

225g jasmine rice

2 tbsp vegetable oil

2 tsp fine sea salt

250–500g leftover cooked turkey and bones

15 dried shrimp, chopped

3 spring onions, halved

3 slices of fresh ginger, thinly sliced on the bias

2 litres water

ground white pepper

TO SERVE:

a drizzle of sesame oil

thinly sliced spring onions

If you're using the raw peanuts, the first thing you need to do is soak them in a small bowl of cold water for 24 hours, then drain.

Rinse the rice three times, until the water runs clear, then drain and mix it with the vegetable oil and salt. Put in a pot with the turkey and bones, chopped dried shrimp, spring onions, ginger and the drained peanuts (if using) and cover with the water. Bring to the boil over a high heat, then cover the pot with a lid, reduce the heat to low and simmer for 1¾ hours. Stir occasionally and add water when the rice starts to stick to the bottom of the pot.

Remove the pot from the heat. Add another 250ml water, then cover with a lid and let the congee steep for an additional hour.

To serve, reheat the congee until it's piping hot. Add ground white pepper to taste and top with the garnishes.

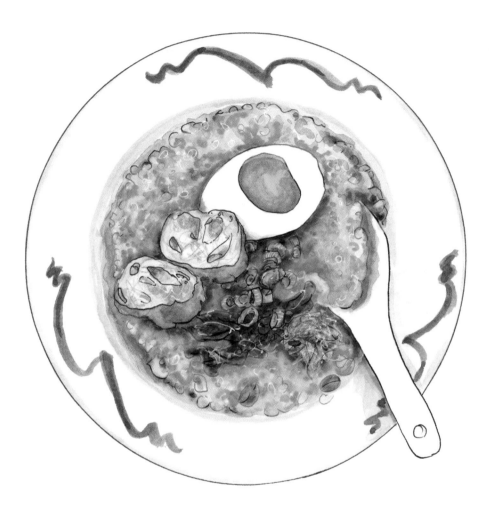

youtiao (Chinese savoury
pastry; see the glossary) or
Yorkshire puddings

salted duck eggs (see the
glossary)

Chinese zha cai (pickled
mustard leaves; see the
glossary)

Chinese rousong (pork floss;
see the glossary)

ONE THOUSAND ZHOUS

There are a thousand zhous out there. My northern
Chinese mother prefers it pure white, which she calls
xi fan – it's just rice with water. My southern friends like
theirs with dried seafood, salt pork and an amber-hued,
green-yolked, lye-preserved century egg. There is fish
zhou, zhou with oatmeal and the Fujian and Taiwan zhou,
simmered and sweet with seafood like crab.

SOUP SPOONS

When it comes to eating and drinking soup, the spoon you use is as important as the ingredients in terms of taste and identifying where your soup is from.

There is a reason we don't eat soup with a teaspoon. Apart from the obvious – the time it would take to consume it – the size of the spoon would hinder you from getting the perfect mouthful of all the elements in your bowl. This is important when you have a soup with lots of ingredients and liquid.

In Europe, the **traditional soup spoon** is oval and ballooned to a depth that adequately allows for a good measure of ingredients and liquid to be scooped up at the same time, and because it's oval, it fits perfectly into your mouth. A **bouillon spoon** is round, much shallower and is used for light or blended soups. There is also a **cream spoon** that is round and its depth and length fall somewhere between these other two. This is also known as a **gumbo spoon**, used for chunky dishes like chowder. In Spain, dishes eaten with spoons are called platos de cuchara, which translates literally as 'spoon dishes'.

In Asia, there are two main types of spoons. The **Chinese spoon** is easily recognisable: a slender, oval-shaped spoon with a flat bottom and a handle that can almost hook your finger. These are traditionally made from porcelain. They are used in countries throughout Asia and are particularly good for soups with dumplings or larger ingredients. The **sujeo**, or **Korean spoon**, has a bowl similar to a bouillon spoon with a longer handle, finding its home in soups or rice. It is often used with chopsticks (in parts of Asia, chopsticks are always served with soup, for example the Vietnamese dish pho).

In Morocco, harira, which is typically eaten every evening after the daily fast of Ramadan ends, has its own specific spoon. Traditionally the olive oil, lentils and vermicelli are measured out in a round-basined **harira spoon**, which is also used to eat the soup afterwards.

HYLDEBÆRSUPPE
DANISH ELDERBERRY SOUP

Majken Bech-Bailey, Demark

SERVES 2

The first time I tasted syrups and drinks made by Majken Bech-Bailey was in the two-Michelin-star restaurant Aimsir in Kildare, where she is general manager. She spoke of her love of foraging and how inspired she is by Irish wild food. Majken's knowledge is astounding and her stories of foraging are romantic. It's not surprising that the recipe Majken has shared is for soup with elderberries, something commonly foraged in both Ireland and Denmark, where she's from (a town called Nakskov on a little island in the south called Lolland).

Majken says, 'My grandmother always made me this soup in the summer and it's among my favourite things to eat during the season. It's just one of the best things to enjoy on a warm summer night.' While I had never tried a warm fruit soup before, I absolutely love this. I can't deny it's partly because it brings back memories of drinking hot Ribena growing up, but it's also divinely reminiscent of fruit crumble in liquid form. – DL

2 slices of Irish brown soda bread

30g light brown sugar

400ml elderberry cordial or juice, concentrated and sweet (see the glossary)

400ml water

20g cornflour

zest and juice of ½ lemon

TO SERVE:

100ml Greek yogurt or crème fraîche

1 apple, diced into very small cubes

Preheat the oven to 130°C fan.

Put the brown bread in a food processor and pulse until it's broken down into fine crumbs, then stir in the brown sugar with a spoon. Transfer to a baking tray and bake in the oven for about 15 minutes, until crisp. Set aside and allow to cool.

Put the elderberry cordial or juice and 300ml of the water in a saucepan. Heat it slowly on a medium-low heat until it's boiling.

Whisk the cornflour with the remaining 100ml of water in a small bowl, then add this to the pan with the elderberry cordial or juice. Bring to the boil, then reduce the heat and simmer for 3 minutes. Adjust the consistency of the soup with a little more water and cordial or juice if it's too thick or with more cornflour if it's too thin. Season with the lemon zest and juice.

Serve the hot soup in bowls finished with a spoonful of Greek yogurt or crème fraîche on top and the crisp brown bread mix and diced apple sprinkled over.

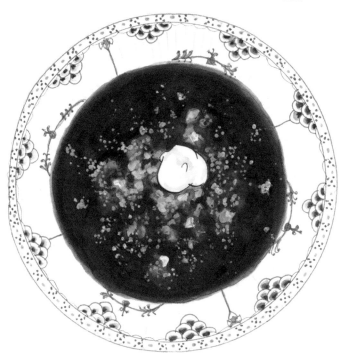

MAKE YOUR OWN

MAKE YOUR OWN
ELDERBERRY SYRUP

Elderberries grow on the elder tree and are in season in Ireland in the autumn. Majken says, 'The best time to harvest elderberries is between mid-August and mid-September. They have to be completely black and soft when you press them.'

You can find elder trees all over the countryside and the berries grow in bunches or clusters. The berries have excellent immune-boosting properties and they have been used for medicinal purposes historically in Ireland.

Never eat them raw, however, as they are poisonous until cooked. They have a tart taste so they make delicious syrup, cordial and juice. 'I will always recommend making elderberry cordial yourself. It is important that you cook them in water with caster sugar to make the cordial,' Majken says. If you want to try making your own elderberry cordial, here's our recipe.

MAKES APPROX. 750ML

1kg elderberries
caster sugar

Pick all the berries off their stems and wash well. Put the berries in a pot and cover with water. Bring to the boil, then reduce the heat and simmer for about 20 minutes, until the berries are soft. Strain into a non-reactive bowl through a fine mesh sieve, a jelly bag or a clean muslin, pushing on the berries with a wooden spoon to extract as much juice as possible.

Now measure the juice – for every 500ml juice, add 450g sugar. Place the juice and the sugar back in the pot over a high heat, stirring to dissolve the sugar. Bring to the boil and allow to boil for 10 minutes. Pour the syrup into clean, sterilised bottles and seal. The syrup can be stored in the fridge for up to a year or you could pour it into an ice cube tray and freeze it, then pop the cubes out and store them in a freezerproof bag in the freezer.

MERCIMEK ÇORBASI
TURKISH RED LENTIL SOUP

Ahmet Dede, Turkey

SERVES 4

Michelin-starred chef Ahmet Dede is nothing short of inspirational. When he arrived in Ireland, not only was he not a chef, but he didn't even know what the Michelin Guide was. Fast forward 10 years and he had been awarded a Michelin star twice – the second time for his own restaurant, Dede in Baltimore, West Cork, which serves food with flavours from Turkey using local produce. Specifically, Ahmet drew from his food memories growing up in Ankara and his mum's cooking. This soup is a dish that Ahmet's mum would cook for him. 'It always reminds me of home,' he says. A bowl of this creamy, blended lentil soup will transport you to the fragrant spice markets of Turkey while nourishing your soul. – DL

1 tbsp vegetable oil

1 onion, chopped

2 garlic cloves, chopped

150g dried red lentils, rinsed

20g tomato purée

1 tsp ground cumin

1 tsp paprika

½ tsp chilli flakes

½ tsp ground black pepper

¼ tsp dried mint

1 litre chicken stock

fine sea salt

TO SERVE:

juice of 1 lemon

natural yogurt

Heat the oil in a large saucepan over a low heat. Add the onion and garlic and sauté for about 5 minutes, until the onion has softened but not coloured.

Add the red lentils and cook for 1 minute, then add the tomato purée and all the spices and dried mint and cook for 1 more minute.

Pour in the stock and bring to the boil, then reduce the heat and simmer for about 20 minutes, until the lentils are soft and the liquid has reduced by half. Blend the soup to a smooth purée, then season to taste with salt.

Serve with a drizzle of lemon juice and a dollop of yogurt on top.

TO FREEZE OR NOT TO FREEZE?

The contents of freezers can possibly tell you more about your friends' habits than their pantry or fridge can. It's not uncommon to have a selection of unrecognisable items in our freezers that ultimately have to be thrown out.

Some soups take well to freezing, especially blended soups, whereas others, sadly, are irreparably damaged by it. Don't freeze soups with vegetables that have a high water content, chopped potatoes, pasta or cheese. If you know you're going to freeze a soup, go easy on the salt because reheating it (and the reduction in liquid that results) will further concentrate the saltiness. Soups from this book that freeze successfully are harira, gazpacho, tom jued (without the tofu), Trinidadian corn soup, Turkish red lentil soup and any stocks. You can also freeze the base for the Mexican tortilla soup and the zazharka for Ukrainian borsch.

Tips:

- Label the storage container with the date and contents.
- Leave 2.5cm of space between the soup and the lid, as liquids expand when they freeze.
- Make sure meats are covered in liquid.
- Use square stackable containers that maximise freezer space.

MOQUECA BAIANA
BAHIA FISH STEW
Euzana Forkan, Brazil

SERVES 4

This stew from Bahia in Brazil captures the essence of the state with its abundant coconuts, fish and azeite de dendê, an unrefined red palm oil that both colours and flavours food. Dendê oil, a native African ingredient, is crucial in the religious offerings that are cooked for the local deities of Candomblé, an Afro-Brazilian religion. This recipe is a staple at MA Gastronomy graduate Euzana Forkan's home in Dublin. Originally from Bahia, Euzana grew up in São Paulo missing her Bahian grandmother's farm and her food. According to Euzana, 'The origin of the moqueca is the result of indigenous, African and Portuguese influences, mixing techniques and ingredients in an authentic national dish.' Euzana recommends playing the quintessential song about missing Bahia, 'Saudade de Bahia', by Antonio Carlos Jobim and Dorival Caymmi when preparing this dish. – BV

2 tbsp extra virgin olive oil

2 white onions, halved and sliced

2 red peppers, sliced

2 yellow peppers, sliced

2 large tomatoes, halved and sliced

fine sea salt and freshly ground black pepper

1 fresh red chilli, deseeded and chopped

1 x 400ml tin of organic coconut milk

2 tbsp azeite de dendê (see the glossary)

500g cod fillets, cut into large pieces

juice of 1 lime

2 tbsp chopped fresh coriander leaves

TO SERVE:

steamed or boiled white rice

1 lime, cut into wedges

Heat 1 tablespoon of the olive oil in a medium heavy-based pot with a lid over a medium-low heat. Add the onions, peppers and tomatoes in alternating layers, seasoning each layer with salt and pepper to taste. Sprinkle the top with the chopped red chilli, then pour in the coconut milk and the red palm oil. Cover the pot with a lid and cook for 15 minutes, until the vegetables are cooked.

Meanwhile, put the fish chunks in a large bowl, drizzle over the lime juice, season with 1 teaspoon salt and toss to coat. Set the fish aside to marinate for 5 minutes, then carefully place the cod fillets on top of the vegetables. Cover the pot with the lid again, bring back to a simmer and cook for about 5 minutes, until the fish is cooked through.

Remove the pot from the heat and drizzle in the remaining tablespoon of olive oil and sprinkle with the chopped coriander. Taste and adjust the seasoning if necessary.

Serve immediately with steamed or boiled white rice and lime wedges for squeezing over.

PASSATELLI IN BRODO
ITALIAN BREADCRUMB PASTA IN BROTH

Gabriele Recchia, Italy

SERVES 2

Gabriele and his brother Matteo, who are originally from Cremona in Lombardy, opened Ripasso in Bray, County Wicklow. A chic Italian restaurant that uses both Italian and Irish high-quality produce, it also has an online Italian produce store. Passatelli is a basic breadcrumb pasta made with eggs and cheese and flavoured with lemon zest and nutmeg. Gabriele says this dish from Emilia-Romagna 'is difficult to find on restaurant menus, even in Italy. Passatelli is perhaps disregarded because of its simplicity or poor origins, but this minestra is perfect as a meal, especially in autumn or winter or any cold rainy day in Ireland.' According to Gabriele, this recipe feeds two – or one hungry Italian. – BV

100g fine breadcrumbs (see the tip)

100g Parmigiano-Reggiano cheese, finely grated, plus extra to serve

10g plain flour, plus extra for dusting

zest of ½ lemon

⅛ tsp ground nutmeg

a pinch of fine sea salt

2 large eggs (ideally free-range or organic)

600ml chicken stock

freshly ground black pepper

Put the breadcrumbs in a large bowl. Add the cheese, flour (this helps to hold the shape), lemon zest, nutmeg and a pinch of salt. Make a well in the middle, then crack the eggs into the well.

Beat the eggs with a fork, then bring all the ingredients together using your hands until you have a crumbly texture. Keep kneading until you can form a soft, pliable ball of dough. Dust a baking tray with a little flour.

Test a piece of dough by placing it in a potato ricer to make sure you can 'rice' it. If it's too dry, add a little stock to the dough. If it's too wet, add more breadcrumbs and knead lightly. When it's just right, divide the dough into four parts.

Bring your stock to a very gentle simmer in a large pot.

Run each piece of dough through a potato ricer, using the disc with the largest openings. Use a sharp knife to cut the dough into 5cm-long strings as the dough comes out of the ricer and place on the floured tray. The pasta will look like thin dumplings. Make sure you clean out any extra dough from the ricer after each use. You can also use a potato masher (the kind with holes in it) to make the passatelli, but it will be a little more difficult.

TRY THIS

Gabriele uses Italian or Polish breadcrumbs (bulka tarta) or makes his own, but never panko (too coarse, as I found out) or golden breadcrumbs (too gritty). I love using Polish bulka tarta in this recipe, a cross-cultural ingredient that is a nod to Ireland's largest international community.

Working in batches, drop the passatelli directly into the simmering broth. Cook gently just until they rise to the top, taking them out straightaway with a slotted spoon and putting them in two bowls. If the stock is too hot or boiling, the passatelli will disintegrate.

Serve the passatelli immediately with the hot broth, a few twists of freshly ground black pepper and extra grated cheese on top.

RASAM
INDIAN LENTIL & TAMARIND SOUP
Asheesh Dewan, India

SERVES 2

It's hard to believe that when Asheesh Dewan came to Ireland in 1995, you couldn't source coriander here – it had to be imported. Almost two decades later, Ireland is known for a remarkably high standard of Indian cuisine. As the owner of Jaipur Group, a portfolio of four award-winning restaurants, Asheesh has played a significant role in our Indian food culture. A legacy of culinary stars has emerged from his business over the years. Asheesh is sophisticated and knowledgeable and his kindness is far-reaching in the industry; many of us are grateful recipients of his friendship.

For Asheesh, rasam is the perfect soup. He says, 'Rasam has neither an authentic nor one original recipe – so for the diehard traditionalist, an apology in advance. Each household has its own recipe. One can begin a meal with hot rasam, other times mop it up with steaming hot rice or use it to thin out a bit of curd rice. It's in its most venerable form when it's consumed when one's feeling a bit under the weather. It's revered like an elixir of life in the entire southern Indian subcontinent. Eat it, drink it, worship it or glorify it, but never wait for the first signs of a cold to make it.' – DL

FOR THE RASAM PODI (BASE POWDER)*:

40g arhar dal (split pigeon peas; see the glossary)

1 tbsp sesame oil, preferably cold-pressed

1½ tbsp black peppercorns

3 tbsp coriander seeds

2 tbsp cumin seeds

1 tbsp ground turmeric

1 tsp chilli powder

*This amount of podi makes three batches of rasam – you need only 40g for this recipe.

It's best to soak the entire amount of arhar dal you need for this recipe (put the 40g for the rasam podi and 30g for the rasam itself in two separate bowls) a day before you plan on beginning. If you are shorter on time, you can soak them for 1 hour beforehand. Either way, it's important to soak them in just-boiled water for at least 1 hour and dry them before using.

To make the rasam podi, heat a heavy-based pan over a low heat. Add the sesame oil and let it heat up for 2 minutes, then increase the heat to medium. Add the soaked and dried arhar dal and toast for about 2 minutes, until they turn a nutty colour. Add the peppercorns, followed by the coriander and cumin seeds. Toast for roughly 2 minutes more, until they are coloured but without scorching them. Let the mixture cool before grinding the arhar dal and seeds to a fine powder. Mix in the turmeric and chilli powder and set aside.

Meanwhile, to make the rasam soup base, soak the tamarind paste in 200ml just-boiled water for 20 minutes. Pour into a bowl through a fine mesh sieve to remove any tamarind fibres and set the water aside.

FOR THE RASAM SOUP BASE:

30g arhar dal

20g tamarind paste (see the glossary)

10g ghee (see the glossary)

¼ tsp asafoetida powder (see the glossary)

2 vine-ripened cherry tomatoes, halved

2 sprigs of fresh coriander

fine sea salt

FOR THE TADKA (TEMPERING):

15g ghee

1 whole dried red chilli, deseeded (optional)

3 fresh curry leaves

1¼ tsp black mustard seeds

2 vine-ripened cherry tomatoes, halved

TO SERVE (OPTIONAL):

2 sprigs of fresh coriander, leaves picked

steamed or boiled white rice (optional)

Put the soaked and dried arhar dal in a small saucepan over a medium-high heat with 275ml water. Cook for about 15 minutes, until they are a watery, mushy consistency.

Heat the ghee in a separate large saucepan over a medium heat until it's just below the smoking point, then take the pan off the heat. Add the asafoetida and cook for about 30 seconds, just until the aroma turns sweet. Put the pan back on a medium heat and add 40g of the rasam podi. Cook for 1 minute, then stir in the tamarind water. Bring to the boil and cook for about 5 minutes, until the raw smell of tamarind has gone.

Add the cooked arhar dal, cherry tomatoes and coriander sprigs. Simmer for 5–7 minutes, until the tomatoes have softened and all the ingredients have infused together, then remove the pan from the heat. Add more water if it has thickened too much – the consistency should be brothy. Add salt to taste. You can remove the coriander sprigs if you like. Keep warm.

To make the tadka, melt the ghee in a small pan over a medium heat. Add the whole dried red chilli (if using), curry leaves and mustard seeds. Cook for about 30 seconds, until the mustard seeds start to pop, then take the pan off the heat. Add the cherry tomatoes, then scrape the tadka into the hot rasam soup base and stir well.

To serve, divide the rasam between two bowls and garnish with coriander leaves. Enjoy on its own as a soup or with a bowl of steaming hot rice.

   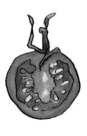 

SABA NO MISOSHIRU
JAPANESE MACKEREL MISO SOUP

Junko Hamilton, Japan

SERVES 2

When Kyoto native Junko Hamilton moved to Howth in Dublin, she could not get the miso she wanted – the fermented paste that is usually made from soybeans but can also be made from barley and rice. A few years later, she became a much-lauded miso teacher in Ireland. For Junko – and indeed, for many Japanese people – miso soup is essential, something that one would have for breakfast every day. She has created 100 miso soups to keep this dish relevant.

Junko has since moved back to her grandmother's house, who sadly passed away at the age of 100. The house is in Kyōtango, outside of Kyoto, a city famed for the longevity of its residents. 'It's all about the fermentation,' Junko explains. – MC

5g kombu (see the glossary)

500ml water

50g daikon radish, peeled and cut into thin sticks

1 mackerel fillet, skin on, cut into four pieces

10g Hatcho or Mame miso (or substitute with aka (red) miso; see the glossary)

10g brown miso

TO GARNISH:

1 spring onion, thinly julienned

a small piece of fresh ginger, peeled and thinly julienned

To make the kombu stock, soak the kombu in the water overnight. The next day, strain the stock and discard the kombu. Boil the stock in a small pot, then add the daikon radish. Cook for a few minutes, then add the mackerel pieces and continue cooking for another few minutes.

Put the Hatcho or Mame miso in a small bowl and add some stock from the pot to dissolve it. Add the miso to the pot and cook for 1 minute.

Put the brown miso in a small bowl and again, add some stock from the pot to dissolve it. Turn off the heat, then add the brown miso to the pot and stir it in.

Divide the soup between two bowls and garnish with the spring onion and ginger.

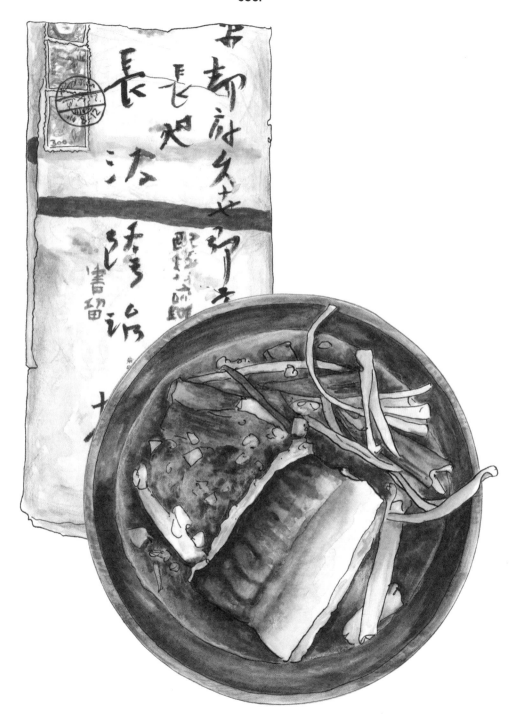

THE STOCK MARKET

According to *Larousse Gastronomique*, a stock contains mostly bone, which has gelatin. If you use mostly meat, the soup becomes a broth or a bouillon. Shop-bought stocks are great, but if you have the time or want to save some money, we definitely recommend making your own. Here are some to try.

CHICKEN STOCK

This is the perfect understudy, for it can be used in many recipes when other stocks are unavailable. There are so many variations, from the one that you make from Sunday chicken's carcass to a golden elixir that you coax from an entire bird, like Jewish chicken-in-the-pot. For a go-to chicken stock, put your leftover roast chicken carcasses (bones and meat) in a heavy-based pot with some oil and place it over a high or medium-high heat. Add 2 onions, 1 leek, 1 carrot and 1 celery stalk, all roughly chopped. Add 1 bunch of fresh parsley, 2 sprigs of thyme, 2 bay leaves, a scant handful of peppercorns and 200ml wine and let the alcohol reduce. Add enough water to cover. Bring to a boil, then reduce the heat to medium-low or low and simmer with the lid off for 1–2 hours, skimming off any froth. Top up the stock with water when needed. Strain and season to taste with salt and pepper.

For a subtler stock or 'white' stock, put 500g raw chicken necks, backs and wings in a pot with vegetables and cover with water. Bring to a boil, then reduce to a simmer and cook for 30–40 minutes.

BEEF STOCK

Beef has to be the star of stocks because you cannot substitute it in recipes that call for other ones. It should be luscious and rich. It can also be high maintenance. Use it for borscht, beef and barley soup, soupe à l'oignon or a consommé. Brown 2kg beef shanks, 1 shin bone and an optional oxtail – you may have to do this in two batches. Add your choice of vegetables (turnip, celery, carrot and onion are all good) and cover with water. Bring to a boil, then reduce the heat and simmer for 2–6 hours. Chill overnight to remove the fat on top. If you separate the meat from the shank after 2 hours and return the bones to the pot, the meat is delicious.

VEGETABLE STOCK

We 'beef up' this stock with mushrooms that have been sautéed and we add more vegetables. Mushrooms contain both amino acids and sugars, thus causing a Maillard reaction. Sauté 300g mushrooms, 2 carrots, 2 onions and 2 leeks, all roughly chopped. Tomato purée is a great addition. Add 200ml white wine and let the alcohol reduce, then add enough water to cover. Simmer for 30 minutes and strain.

FISH STOCK

Fish stock needs to be cooked only briefly, otherwise it becomes unpleasantly bitter. Use 500g fish bones and heads (ask your fishmonger). You can also add shells and the heads of shrimp and/or lobster. Add your choice of vegetables (we love leek and diced fennel). Add 200ml white wine and let the alcohol reduce, then add water to cover and simmer for 20 minutes. Chill overnight and remove any fat that comes to the surface.

DASHI

For an alternative vegetarian stock, soak 5g kombu in 500ml water overnight. If you add 10g dried bonito flakes (see the glossary) with the kombu, it becomes a delicious fish stock. Bring the broth to a boil, then strain the stock. Dashi provides the base for soups like miso (see Junko Hamilton's mackerel miso soup on page 44), but it also imparts a fragrance to rice, ramen and omelettes.

BROWN, BLOND OR BLANCH?

When meat or bones are browned, it creates a Maillard reaction: a chemical reaction between amino acids and reducing sugars that gives browned food its distinctive flavour. The amino acids and sugar become umami, that mysterious glutamate-rich savour that is present in Parmesan, cooked tomatoes and anchovies. We brown our ingredients because it yields a richer-tasting soup in a shorter amount of time, but you can skip the browning, simmer and skim more patiently and have a subtler-tasting product that is 'blond'. Moreover, there are stocks in certain countries (like those in South-East and East Asia) that require blanching, where you boil the bones, strain them and scrub them of blood and impurities, then return the bones to the pot with clean water.

TRY THIS

We love using an electric pressure cooker, like an Instant Pot, for stocks as it's a one-pot solution that not only saves time but energy too (see page 26).

SINIGANG NA HIPON
FILLIPINO TAMARIND SOUP WITH SHRIMP

John Bueno, Philippines

SERVES 4

John Bueno, executive chef at the Guinness Storehouse, shared this recipe as it was the first dish he learned to cook as a precocious culinary child, so it's close to his heart. Sinigang na hipon is a tamarind broth with vegetables and shrimp and is a little similar to Thai tom yum. Its sourness is its badge of honour and it can be had at any time of the day. Tamarind is a versatile ingredient that can be used in sweet and savoury preparations and one that Mei, Dee and I all love, whether as a drink, a candy (Mexican Pulparindo) or in this soup. It pairs perfectly with chilli. You can adjust the tartness by using more or less tamarind powder and adjust the heat by doubling the amount of chilli called for. – BV

2 small ripe tomatoes, cut into quarters

2 small onions, cut into quarters

1 fresh green finger chilli, deseeded and halved lengthways or to taste

1½ tbsp fish sauce, plus extra to serve

a pinch of freshly ground black pepper

1.25 litres water

2 tbsp Sampalok Mix Original Tamarind Powder (see the glossary)

½ small daikon radish, peeled and sliced

150g snake beans or green beans, cut into 7.5cm-long pieces

150g okra, sliced in half at an angle

500g tiger prawns, shell on and deveined

150g kangkong (leaves and stems separated; see the glossary) or kale leaves, thinly sliced

Put the tomatoes, onions, chilli, fish sauce and a pinch of freshly ground black pepper in a large pot and pour in the water. Cover the pot and bring to the boil, then reduce the heat and simmer for 5–7 minutes, until the onions are soft.

Stir in the tamarind powder, then add the daikon, snake or green beans and the okra. Simmer for 5–7 minutes, until the vegetables are cooked.

Add the tiger prawns and simmer for another 2 minutes, then add the kangkong and cook for 1 minute more. (If using kale, add it before the tiger prawns.)

Ladle into bowls. Serve with jasmine rice on the side and the bottle of fish sauce as a condiment to add to taste.

TO SERVE:

steamed or boiled jasmine rice

SOONDOOBU
KOREAN TOFU HOT POT

Soonie Delap, Korea

SERVES 4

When Soonie Delap arrived in Ireland in the 1980s, there were few Asians and even fewer Koreans, but like so many of us foreign women, she had fallen for an Irishman. Soonie, a hospital social worker, quickly established the Korean School Dublin and over the years has become the de facto ambassador of all things Korean, including food. Armed with a fabulous kitchen and impeccable taste, Soonie is a legendary hostess. This stew of soft pillowy egg tofu and earthy mushrooms cooked in a chilli broth is served in individual bowls and is a popular option both in restaurants and at home. It captures the essence of Korean home cooking and Soonie's entertaining style. – BV

1 tbsp vegetable oil

400g pork mince, preferably loin

1 leek, finely chopped

1 tbsp gochugaru (Korean chilli powder; see the glossary)

1 tbsp soy sauce

2 tsp finely chopped garlic

400ml water

400g soft tofu or silken egg tofu, sliced (see the tip and the glossary)

100g shiitake mushrooms, sliced

100g enoki mushrooms, pulled apart

1 tbsp fish sauce

1 tsp sesame oil

fine sea salt and freshly ground black pepper

TO SERVE:

steamed or boiled rice

kimchi (see the glossary)

Heat the oil in a pot over a medium heat. When it's hot, add the pork mince and stir-fry until lightly browned. Add the leek and stir-fry for a couple minutes, then add the gochugaru, soy sauce and garlic and stir-fry for 1 minute.

Pour in the water and bring to the boil, then add the tofu, shiitake and enoki mushrooms, fish sauce and sesame oil and simmer for 2 minutes. Season to taste with salt and pepper.

Serve immediately with steamed or boiled rice and a little side of kimchi.

SILKEN EGG TOFU

Sold in a cylindrical package, silken egg tofu is often pan-fried and served in a sauce, such as sweet chilli sauce or mushroom sauce, or steamed with a dash of sesame oil, soy sauce and grated ginger.

SOPA DE TORTILLA
MEXICAN TORTILLA SOUP
Julian Trejo Pascual, Mexico

SERVES 4

Julian Trejo Pascual, his mother, Maribel, and brother, Francisco, run the popular taco food truck El Milagro. We adore their clever hashtag #taqueromucho, a word play on te quiero (I love you) and taquero (a person who makes or eats tacos). Find them at food markets, festivals and pop-ups all over Dublin. Their takes on traditional tacos like beef birria and chicken tinga are some of the most flavourful you can find in the capital city. His recipe is a fancier version of sopa de tortilla, an everyday soup that uses day-old tortillas in an ancho chilli tomato broth garnished with cheese, avocado, tortilla chips and lime juice. As if we needed more reasons to love Mexican food. – BV

2 dried ancho chillies (see the glossary)

20 soft small corn tortillas, cut into thin strips

sunflower oil, for deep-frying

1 tbsp vegetable oil

5 tomatoes, chopped, or 1 x 400g tin of chopped tomatoes

1 small white onion, chopped

1 garlic clove, chopped

1 litre vegetable stock

2 bay leaves

1½ tsp fine sea salt

TO SERVE:

1 avocado

250g feta, cubed

180g crème fraîche

1–2 limes, cut into wedges

Cut the ancho chillies in half lengthways and deseed them, then cut into thin strips. This will be easier if the chilli is soft and pliable, but harder if it's very dry.

Reserve a quarter of the chilli strips and tortilla strips. Set aside.

Pour the sunflower oil into a heavy-based pot suitable for deep-frying, making sure the pot is no more than half full. Alternatively, you can use a dedicated deep-fryer. Either way, heat the oil to 180°C.

Working in batches, deep-fry the tortilla strips for about 2 minutes, until light golden brown. Transfer carefully to a baking tray lined with kitchen paper to absorb any excess oil.

Next, deep-fry the ancho chilli strips for just 5 seconds, being careful not to burn them. You want them to be nice and crisp. Drain on the kitchen paper.

Heat the tablespoon of vegetable oil in a pot over a medium heat. Add the tomatoes and onion and cook for 5 minutes, stirring often, until soft. Add the garlic and cook for 1 minute. Add the reserved chilli and tortilla strips to the pot and cook, stirring, for a couple of minutes.

MAKE IT MIDWEEK

An easy-breezy midweek version of this soup is to substitute the tortillas for plain (unflavoured, please!) tortilla chips (or totopos, as they are called in Mexico). Skip frying the chillies – soak them in water for 30 minutes, then chop them and cook them with the tomatoes and onion.

Take the pot off the heat. Transfer the mix to a blender or food processor and blitz to a purée, then add back to the pot along with the vegetable stock, bay leaves and salt. Cover with a lid and bring to the boil, then reduce the heat and simmer for 10 minutes, stirring occasionally.

Meanwhile, peel, stone and slice the avocado. When the soup is done, remove the bay leaves and taste to check the seasoning.

Ladle the soup into bowls and garnish with the fried tortilla and chilli strips, avocado slices, feta and a dollop of crème fraîche, with lime wedges on the side for squeezing over.

SOUPE À L'OIGNON
FRENCH ONION SOUP

Thomas Loisel, France

SERVES 4

Thomas Loisel, head chef at Dublin's Piglet Wine Bar, grew up in the bucolic village of Noyers-sur-Serein outside Chablis in France. His take on traditional French onion soup is redolent of thyme and garlic. Like his mother, he puts a grating of Comté at the bottom of the bowl for a sublime stretch of cheese in each spoon. It is seductive and cosy – just like the best onion soups want to be – and worth the heartburn that may ensue. – MC

40g butter

4 medium onions, very thinly sliced

1 litre high-quality shop-bought beef stock

100ml white wine

2 garlic cloves, thinly sliced

2 bay leaves

1 sprig of fresh thyme, leaves only

fine sea salt and freshly ground black pepper

TO FINISH:

8 baguette slices, sliced at an angle into pieces about 2cm thick

2 garlic cloves, halved

200g Comté cheese, grated

Melt the butter in a large heavy-based saucepan over a medium heat. Add the onions along with a splash of water. Cook, stirring occasionally, until the onions are browned and caramelised. Take care not to let them burn, adding a splash of water if necessary to prevent them from catching on the bottom of the pan. This will take anywhere between 40 minutes and 1 hour. The time will vary depending on your pan, the thickness of your onions and the heat source.

Meanwhile, put the beef stock, wine, garlic, bay leaves and thyme in a separate heavy-based pot over a medium heat. Simmer for 20 minutes, then strain the liquid, disposing of the garlic and herbs. Season to taste – the stock should be slightly salty and full of umami.

Add the strained stock to the onions and continue to simmer for 15 minutes. Season again with salt and pepper.

Preheat the grill to medium-high.

To assemble, toast the baguette slices in a pan or under the grill, then rub vigorously with the halved garlic cloves. Discard the garlic.

Pour a ladleful of soup into each of four heatproof bowls, then add a sprinkle of the Comté. Add two or three more ladles of the soup, then top each bowl with two baguette slices and shower with Comté cheese. Put the bowls under the grill for approximately 5 minutes, until the toast and cheese are browned and slightly puffed.

TOM JUED
THAI CLEAR BROTH WITH MEATBALLS

Nan Srakhunthod, Thailand

SERVES 2

Dublin-born chef Nan Srakhunthod has worked in Pichet restaurant and the now-closed Bangkok-based two-Michelin-star Indian restaurant Gaggan, but her Thai roots run deep. Her family co-founded Baan Thai in 1998, the year she was born. Growing up, Nan spent summers in Issan with her family. These days, Nan assuages bouts of Issan homesickness with her mother's shrimp relish and lashings of her favourite herb, coriander, with the roots attached. Nan says, 'We pick it when it's young. The root is so tender, you just eat the whole thing.' Nan introduced us to tom jued: meatballs, tofu and Chinese cabbage suspended in a transparent broth. It's a mainstay on many Thai menus, a subtle sip at the start of the meal to balance the often pungent, complicated heat to follow. – MC

FOR THE MEATBALLS:

40g mung bean vermicelli noodles (see the glossary)

200g pork mince

15g fresh coriander stalks, finely chopped

fine sea salt and ground white pepper

FOR THE BROTH:

600ml water

1 small white onion, thinly sliced

2 garlic cloves, finely minced

3 tbsp Golden Mountain Seasoning Sauce or Healthy Boy thin soy sauce (see the tip and the glossary)

½ tsp powdered chicken bouillon (optional)

To make the pork meatballs, first soak the vermicelli in hot water for 30 minutes, then drain and chop into 2cm pieces. Put in a bowl with the pork mince, chopped coriander stalks, salt and white pepper and mix to combine. Roll into small 3cm balls.

To make the broth, bring the water to the boil in a large, heavy-based pot over a medium-high heat. Add the pork meatballs to the boiling water along with the onion, garlic, Golden Mountain seasoning or soy sauce, bouillon (if using), sugar, salt and white pepper.

Once the pork meatballs float up to the surface, turn the heat down to medium-low. Add the Chinese cabbage and tofu and simmer for 3 minutes, until the cabbage and onion are soft.

To serve, ladle the soup into bowls and garnish with coriander leaves, spring onions and fried garlic.

½ tsp caster sugar

½ tsp fine sea salt

a pinch of ground white pepper

200g Chinese cabbage, cut into 3cm squares

150g egg tofu or soft tofu, cut into 3cm cubes (see the glossary)

TO GARNISH:

fresh coriander leaves

spring onions, chopped

1 tsp fried garlic (see the glossary)

TRY THIS

If you can't get Golden Mountain Seasoning Sauce or Healthy Boy thin soy sauce, use 3 tablespoons light soy sauce (preferably Kikkoman) mixed with ½ teaspoon brown sugar.

Tom jued is a delicately flavoured soup, but you can add more water, chicken bouillon or salt to your liking.

TRINIDADIAN CORN SOUP

Alistair 'JD' Jeje, Trinidad

SERVES 6

Corn soup is popular in the Caribbean, including the island of Trinidad. This Trinidadian version was shared with us by Alistair, who is known to all as JD. He's the owner of Socafro Kitchen, his street food business in Waterford City that serves Caribbean and Nigerian takeaway food. The cuisine combination is a result of JD's heritage: his mum is from Trinidad and his dad is from Nigeria. The name Socafro, on the other hand, is a combination of his favourite music: Caribbean soca music and Afro beats. Born in England, JD grew up in Lagos, where his mum and sister taught him how to cook. 'My mother taught me how to blend and meld national dishes from these two continents into one scrumptious meal. I set up this business as I realised that cooking comes naturally to me. I can cook for days. Your gift is what you can do with the least amount of effort, right?' JD is one of those people who immediately imprints on your memory, as his personality is as big and infectious as his smile. This is one of his favourite Trinidadian soups and we guarantee that once you taste it, it will be a favourite of yours too. – DL

900g fresh corn kernels (about 4 cobs)

250ml chicken stock

2 tbsp butter

115g spring onions or fresh chives, chopped

1 sweet red pepper, chopped

½ tsp finely chopped garlic

750ml milk

1 tsp fine sea salt

½ tsp ground white pepper or hot pepper (Scotch bonnet, fresh red chilli pepper or a few dashes of chilli sauce), to taste

TO SERVE:

chopped fresh parsley

toast soldiers

Shave the corn kernels off the cobs, then put them in a blender with the stock and blitz to a purée.

Melt the butter in a large saucepan over a low heat. Add the spring onions or chives, sweet red pepper and garlic and cook for about 2 minutes. Add the corn purée and simmer for 15 minutes, still over a low heat.

Pour the milk into the pan and add the salt and pepper (whichever one you would like to use). Continue to cook for 10 minutes.

Ladle into bowls and garnish with a little chopped fresh parsley. Serve with toast soldiers on the side for dipping.

WATERCRESS SOUP WITH POACHED EGG

Myrtle Allen, Ireland

SERVES 6

Myrtle Allen is called the matriarch of modern Irish cuisine. She devoted her life to advocating for Irish food and its producers and her legacy, Ballymaloe House, is now a beloved institution. We have included only one Irish soup in this book and it had to be Mrs Allen's watercress soup, as iconic to Irish food as the woman herself. I adore this soup, and I adored Mrs Allen. In fact, I had it as a starter for my wedding day lunch in the Intercontinental Hotel Dublin, where it was served poured over a poached egg, an addition which we have opted for here. Thank you to Fern Little, Mrs Allen's daughter, for allowing us to include this cherished recipe. – DL

60g butter

140g potatoes, diced

110g onion, chopped

fine sea salt and freshly ground black pepper

225g watercress, chopped

500ml water

500ml milk

1 egg yolk

1 tbsp thick cream

TO SERVE:

6 eggs (1 per serving)

small watercress sprigs

Melt the butter in a heavy saucepan over a medium heat. When it foams, add the potatoes and onion and toss in the butter until well coated. Sprinkle with salt and pepper, reduce the heat, cover the pan with a lid and sweat for 10 minutes.

Add the watercress, water and milk and simmer for a further 10 minutes.

Mix the egg yolk and cream together in a small bowl. Pour into the soup and turn off the heat while stirring. Don't boil again. Blend the soup.

Poach the eggs in a separate saucepan of water until the whites are cooked but the yolks are still soft. Place a poached egg in each bowl.

To serve, pour the soup through a sieve (to remove any small bits) on top of each egg, being gentle so as not to burst the yolks. Garnish with a few watercress sprigs.

DON'T SWEAT IT!

The cooking term 'sweating' is often misused or confused with 'sautéing', so we wanted to clear up the meaning to stop you sweating it next time you're in a kerfuffle in the kitchen!

SWEATING Cooking chopped vegetables in their own juices in a covered pan over a gentle heat so that they become soft but do not brown. A little fat is usually used to begin the cooking process. Sweating is a popular alternative to sautéing or frying as a low-fat cooking method.

SAUTÉING Cooking meat, fish or vegetables in fat in a pan until brown. Slightly thicker pieces sometimes need to be covered to complete the cooking. The process can consist of frying food while vigorously shaking the pan, preventing it from sticking and ensuring it's cooked on all sides.

GLOSSARY

Africa's Finest Dried Fish

This brand can be found in international shops all over Ireland. They specialise in dried fish that you will find in West African and Asian dishes. In particular, crayfish powder is a dominant flavour in Nigerian sauces and dried lizard fish is added to efo riro (Nigerian spinach stew).

African pure palm oil

Used a lot in West African dishes such as jollof rice, red palm oil adds a smoky flavour that is distinct in this cuisine. Tropical Sun is a good brand of unrefined red palm oil and you can find it in international stores with an African food section.

All-purpose vegetable seasoning

You can use any kind of vegetable seasoning to flavour soups and you'll find them in Polish and international stores. Jumbo Aroma is a good brand of African vegetable seasoning.

Ancho chilli

A dried raisin-sweet and smoky version of a fresh poblano chilli. This mild chilli is used in a myriad of Mexican dishes, such as moles, adobos and salsas.

Arhar dal (split pigeon peas)

Also known as toor dal, these are one of the most popular pulses in India. Yellow in colour, these hulled legumes break down easily when cooked.

Asafoetida powder

A pungent spice, asafoetida is a gum that comes from a variety of giant fennel and is used a lot in Indian dishes. It is often used as a replacement for someone who doesn't eat garlic or onions.

Azeite de dendê (red palm oil)

A crucial ingredient in Brazilian cuisine. It is an unrefined oil extracted from the fruit of the palm tree as opposed to the seeds, which is the case for the refined palm oil. It has a nutty, grassy, pronounced flavour.

Beetroot kvass or beetroot juice concentrate

Kvass is used in borscht and gives it a distinct sour flavour. If using, it's important not to bring it to the boil – simply add it towards the end of the cooking time after taking the pot off the heat. Concentrated beetroot juice makes a good replacement.

Curry leaves

Also known as sweet neem, this tree is native to Asia. You can buy fresh or dried leaves; the fresh add a stronger fragrance. They have highly medicinal properties.

Dried bonito flakes Also known as katsuobushi, these are flakes of skipjack tuna, simmered, smoked and dried.

Elderberry cordial or juice You can find this in health food stores and Polish food shops. There are high-quality organic versions available. Make sure it's concentrated and sweet.

Fried garlic This is a popular garnish in South-East Asia. The most widely available type in Ireland is the Malaysian-manufactured Dollee.

Ghee A clarified butter, available in any international shops. There are even a couple of Irish producers making it now too.

Gochugaru A red chilli pepper mix that ranges from mild to moderately hot. It's a key ingredient in Korean cuisine and is essential to kimchi, gochujang (a fermented pepper paste), stews and soups. Aside from its faint sweet flavour, gochugaru imparts a distinctive red colour to food that is difficult to substitute.

Golden Mountain Seasoning Sauce or Healthy Boy thin soy sauce Available in many Asian markets, these Thai soy sauces differ from Chinese and Japanese brands because they have been sweetened. Golden Mountain also has a 'flavour enhancer' derived from dried fish and/or seaweed for that extra savour.

Guascas A South American herb with a faint flavour of artichoke. In Ireland, guascas is called gallant soldiers and is considered a weed. You can find guascas online in Latin American shops in Spain. Substitute with either coriander and thyme or spinach and dried oregano.

Kangkong A leafy green vegetable that grows on water, also called morning glory or tong cai in Chinese. It can be used in stir-fries or tempura. It wilts very quickly, so consume it straight after purchase. Available in Filipino and Asian stores.

Kimchi A spicy fermented cabbage (or other vegetables) with gochugaru, fish sauce, garlic and ginger. Kimchi has gone from relative obscurity to global stardom and is now both a superfood and a chef-revered ingredient.

Kombu The Japanese word for kelp. This seaweed is used to make the dashi (stock) that is the base of many Japanese soups.

Miso Fermented soybean paste, often sold in a tub. There are many different types of miso made with rice, barley and even seaweed and it comes in a variety of colours: white, brown and red. Miso can be used to make soups, sauces and marinades.

Mung bean vermicelli noodles Mung bean or vermicelli noodles are available in East Asian markets and many mainstream supermarkets. Sometimes labelled as glass noodles or bean thread noodles, they are crystal-hued and very fine. They are a staple in Chinese, Japanese, Vietnamese and Thai cooking.

Nata A thick South American cream with a sour touch. You can order it from Sabanero Artisan Cheese in Galway, a Venezuelan-owned business that uses Irish dairy to make Venezuelan cheeses.

Pepper soup mix Used to make Nigerian pepper soups, which can be made with vegetables, fish or meat. Available in all international stores with African sections.

Rousong (pork floss) A dehydrated meat product that is magic, for this is protein spun into threads. It has a sweet taste and is light and airy. Pastries in China come decorated with pork floss, as do humble zhous. Fancy versions are sold in department stores, where it commands high prices.

Salted duck eggs Duck eggs that have been preserved in salt paste. The whites are custardy and the yolks are oily, crumbly and golden.

Soft or silken tofu This tofu comes packaged in a box or cylinder and is very soft. Some packages will be labelled as soon tofu in Korean versions. You can replace it with Japanese cylindrical silken egg tofu.

Tamarind paste Made from tamarind fruit, a sour, dark, sticky fruit that grows in a pod on a tamarind tree. It can be used in sweet and savoury dishes. You can dissolve the paste in hot water – just make sure to sieve out any bits before adding to your food.

Tamarind powder Made from unripe tamarind pods, this powder comes in three versions: Sinigang sa Sampalok Mix Original for shrimp dishes, Gabi for pork and Miso for salmon or fish. Knorr makes good versions. Available in Filipino stores and multi-country stores like Ingredients in Drogheda, Bray and Stillorgan.

Tkemali A Georgian specialty sauce of green plums, wild mint, coriander and garlic. Considered the Georgian ketchup, it can, like tomato ketchup, be doused on all vegetables and meats. You can find bottled tkemali in the Molodova and Polonez stores around Ireland.

Wild green plums or alycha plums A sour wild plum that is harvested for a brief spring season. Firm and tart, they are paired with chakapuli (Georgian lamb stew). They appear in shops for two weeks in April. Find them at the Ayla, Moldova or Polonez stores.

Youtiao A deep-fried salty pastry that is eaten at breakfast alongside soy milk or zhou. Youtiaos are made from a leavened dough and cut into strips before frying.

Zha cai Dried fermented mustard leaves that have been salted and spiced. Although this ingredient originates from the Sichuan province, it is beloved by Chinese everywhere. It's sold in cans or packets.

Scan for the Spice Bags shopping guide to Dublin's Capel Street area.

INDEX

Nine Bean Rows

23 Mountjoy Square

Dublin, D01 E0F8

Ireland

@9beanrowsbooks

ninebeanrowsbooks.com

NINE
BEAN
ROWS

Blasta Books is an imprint of Nine Bean Rows Books Ltd.

@blastabooks blastabooks.com

First published 2023

Copyright © Blanca Valencia, Dee Laffan and Mei Chin, 2023

ISBN: 978-1-9993799-5-7

Editor: Kristin Jensen

Series artist: Nicky Hooper
nickyhooper.com

Designer: Jane Matthews
janematthewsdesign.com

Proofreader: Jocelyn Doyle

Printed by L&C Printing Group, Poland

The paper in this book is produced using pulp from managed forests.

10 9 8 7 6 5 4 3 2 1

About the authors

Blanca Valencia is a cook, writer, speaker and podcaster. Born in Spain, she grew up in Central America and has lived and worked in the UK, China, France, Argentina, the US and now Ireland. She has a Grand Diplôme from London's Le Cordon Bleu and an MA in Gastronomy from TU Dublin. Her work experience includes running the test kitchens in Books for Cooks (London) and elBulli Hotel (Seville) and running the cooking school at Alambique (Madrid). She collaborates regularly with the Spanish Commercial and Tourism Offices, Spanish wine regions and the Cervantes Institute in the US and Ireland. She is the co-host of the award-winning Spice Bags podcast. Blanca passionately believes in diversity and education through food and her experience includes Common Threads, Purple Asparagus, the City of Madrid and the Chicago Cultural Center.

@blancsvalencia

Dee Laffan is a freelance journalist and editor with over 15 years' experience in the areas of food, drink and travel. Editor-in-chief of Ireland's only long-form food writing magazine, *Scoop*, she is also the former editor of Irish magazines *Food&Wine*, *Easy Food* and *Yes Chef!* and publishing director of the *fft* hospitality title. She has also written for all Irish national newspapers. Dee's work extends to broadcasting, currently co-hosting the Spice Bags podcast – awarded Best Irish Food Podcast by the Irish Food Writing Awards in 2021 – and as a contributor on the *Ireland AM* morning TV show. Her business also includes digital content consultancy, working with clients from the hospitality industry to create and manage digital strategies, content and social media. Dee's passion for Irish food has led her to many roles: co-host of the food stage at Taste of Dublin, host of BasteCamp at the Big Grill Festival and a judge of Blas na hÉireann (Irish Food Awards). Dee is a proud member of the Irish Food Writers' Guild.

@deelaffan